P9-EER-160

HOUGHTON MIFFLIN

Reading

A Legacy of Literacy

We Can Work It Out

HOUGHTON MIFFLIN   BOSTON • MORRIS PLAINS, NJ

California   •   Colorado   •   Georgia   •   Illinois   •   New Jersey   •   Texas

ISBN 0-618-07498-8

3456789-BS-06 05 04 03 02 01 00

Design, Art Management, and Page Production: Studio Goodwin Sturges

Contents

Pet Show

by Mary Gold
illustrated by Pedro Martin

"Let's go see the Oak Tree
Road's Pet Show," said Joan.

"We can see a crow,
a toad, and a goat."

"See that?" asked Joan.
"Rob's goat is eating the
bow on the crow's cage."

"Rob, stop that goat,"
yelled Liz. "He is towing
those pets to Oak Tree Lake."

"Slow down, Oats," yelled Rob.
"Stop! Stop! Stop!"

"I got the crow,"
boasted Rob.

"And I got the toad!"
boasted Liz.

"Where is the goat?"
asked Joan.

"He's eating Rob's coat," Liz moaned.

"No," said Rob. "Oats is just hunting for oats!"

Nick Is Sick

by Tricia Lee
illustrated by Elbrite Brown

"I feel hot," moaned Nick.
"And my throat hurts lots. I
want Mom and Dad."

"Mom and Dad are gone for three days," said Miss Pim, "but I know I can help."

"Go rest in bed," said Miss
Pim.

"Mom makes me rest,"
groaned Nick.

"I can make toast and big bowls of hot broth," said Miss Pim.

"Dad makes me that," croaked Nick.

"Blow on it. Then drink it up,"
said Miss Pim. "You will be well
in no time."

"Mom tells me that," croaked
Nick.

"Let's read a bit," said Miss
Pim.

"Mom and Dad both read
when I am sick," said Nick.

"Miss Pim, it's Mom and Dad,"
said Nick. "I am sick, but Miss
Pim can make me well."

Don's Boat

by Mack Duffy
illustrated by Bill Morrison

"Let's go, Ben," said Jen.
"Don wants to show us
his big boat at the lake."

"Is this the boat, Don?"
asked Ben.

"Yes. We must blow it up,"
said Don. "It's hard, but I
know we can do it."

"Ben and I can help,"
said Jen.

"Yes," said Ben. "We can
help blow up the boat."

"See," said Don. "When we
row, we can make the boat
go fast or slow."

"It's your turn, Ben,"
gasped Jen.

"This is hard," panted Ben.
"Take it, Jen."
"Not yet, please,"
moaned Jen.

"We did it!" boasted Don.
"It floats! Do you want a
boat ride?"

"Yes! Yes!" yelled Jen
and Ben.

"We can take turns rowing," said Don.

"Take turns?" groaned Jen and Ben. "Not that!"

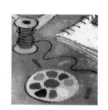

Chan's Gift

by Mack Duffy

illustrated by Tungwai Chau

Chan needed a gift.

"Mom likes to cook," he said.

"I can get Mom a cookbook."

Chan picked up a cookbook at Bill's Books, but it cost too much. Chan just had ten dimes.

"Mom likes to write," Chan said.
"I can get Mom a notebook."

Chan picked up a notebook at Nell's Nook, but the notebook cost too much.

"What book can I get with
ten dimes?" Chan asked
Miss Brook.

"You can make a book,"
she said.

Chan gave Miss Brook ten dimes.
He took home blank pages and
string. He made his own book.

34

"It's a scrapbook, Mom,"
said Chan. "Write in it. Write
things you like to cook!"

Ann Can't Sleep

by Peri Jones
illustrated by Dorothy Donohue

Ann had a hard time going
to sleep.

The wind was blowing. It
shook the treetops. Ann was
afraid. She yelled, "Mom!"

Mom had an idea. She got
books from Ann's bookcase.
She kissed Ann's cheek.

Then the wind made the
woods creak and groan. This
time Ann yelled, "Dad!"

Dad took Ann a big glass of
hot milk. He kissed Ann's cheek.

Raindrops fell and the woods
shook.

Ann yelled, "Matt!"

Matt had a good plan. He took
Ann his stuffed bear. Ann gave
it a big, big hug and went to
sleep!

Rick and Dad Go Camping

by Carly Mackeen
illustrated by Anik McGrory

Rick and Dad packed the truck. Dad packed the tent and sleeping bags. Rick took fishhooks and fishing poles.

"Catch lots of fish,"
yelled Mom.

Dad set up the tent. Rick got
wood and water.

Rick and Dad fished in a
wide brook. No fish came.

"Where are the fish, Dad?"
asked Rick.

"They're not in this brook,"
said Dad.

Upstream, five bears fished
in the wide brook. They ate
lots and lots of fish.

Back at the campsite, Rick
and Dad heated beans on
the campfire.

"We didn't catch any fish,
but we've got lots of beans,"
said Rick.

Clues from Boots

by Tina Mendosa
illustrated by Bill Brandon

"Thank you for keeping
Boots while I go on this trip,"
said Drew. "His clues will let
you know just what to do."

Boots ran up and down. Then
he picked up a stick and gave it
to Sue.

"Is this a clue?" asked Sue.

Sue threw the stick. Boots
jumped up high to get it.
"It was a clue!" cried Sue.

Sue and Boots went inside.
Boots stood by his bowl. He
pushed the bowl with his nose.

"This is a good clue, Boots!"
said Sue. "You need food
and water."

Then Sue gave a clue. She shut
the light to see if Boots would
lie on his bed.

He did!

"Goodnight and sleep tight!" said Sue.

Lou's Tooth

by Chris Petersen
illustrated by Heidi Chang

"My tooth is loose," cried Lou.

"It's true," said Mom. "Good
for you, Lou!"

"It's just an old tooth," said
Lee.

Right at the start of class,
Miss Moon wrote Lou's name
on the loose tooth list. She
gave Lou a patch.

Lou tried to show his new
patch to Lee, but Lee just
looked away.

Lou's group tried to make a big log shed.

"Here is glue for that loose tooth," said Lee.

Lou had pie in his lunch.
"I'll take that. You can't
chew," said Lee. "You should
just eat fish soup."

Lou sighed. Lee was not being nice and Lou knew why. Lee didn't have any loose teeth yet.

Lee fell on the lace of his shoe.

Lee cried, "Look! My tooth is loose!"

Lou felt glad that Lee had a loose tooth, too.

A Clean Room

by Gary Demas
illustrated by Ashley Wolff

"This room is a real mess,"
said Dad. "Clean it up. Then
you and Boo can go play."

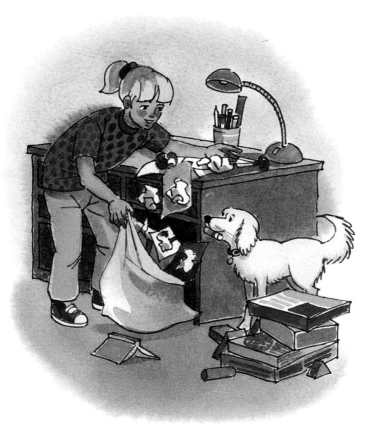

Trish sighed, "Let's start with this desk."

She threw out bits and pieces of cut paper. Boo found her missing glue stick.

Then Trish picked up her
raincoat and ~~green~~ boots. *red*
Boo found Mom's new blue
shoes under the bed.

Trish hung up five hats she
did not like to wear. Boo
found Dad's lost flashlight.

Trish scooped up games and
blocks to build with. Boo found
his best chew bone.

Trish got the broom. She was
very glad when she swept up
three dimes.

"Good job," said Dad. "You
can go play."

"Not right now," sighed Trish.
"It is so nice and clean, I'll
just lie right here and read."

Word Lists

Theme 7, Week 1

Pet Show (p. 5) accompanies *That Toad is Mine!*

Decodable Words

New
Vowel Pairs *oa, ow:* boasted, coat, goat, Joan, moaned, Oak, Oats, Road's, toad, bow, crow, crow's, Show, slow, towing

Previously Taught
and, asked, cage, can, eating, go, got, he, he's, hunting, is, just, Lake, let's, Liz, no, on, Pet, pets, Rob, Rob's, see, stop, that, those, Tree, we, yelled

High-Frequency Words

Previously Taught
a, down, for, I, said, the, to, where

Theme 7, Week 1

Nick Is Sick (p. 13) accompanies *That Toad is Mine!*

Decodable Words

New
Vowel Pairs *oa, ow:* croaked, groaned, moaned, throat, toast, blow, bowl, know

Previously Taught
am, and, be, bed, big, bit, broth, but, can, Dad, days, drink, feel, go, help, hot, in, is, it, it's, let's, lots, make, makes, me, Miss, Mom, Nick, no, on, Pim, read, rest, sick, tells, that, then, three, time, up, well, when, will

High-Frequency Words

New
both, gone, want

Previously Taught
a, are, for, hurts, I, my, of, said, you

Theme 7, Week 1

Don's Boat (p. 21) accompanies *That Toad is Mine!*

Decodable Words

New

Vowel Pairs *oa, ow:* boasted, boat, floats, groaned, moaned, blow, know, row, rowing, show, slow

Previously Taught

and, asked, at, Ben, big, but, can, did, Don, Don's, fast, gasped, go, help, his, is, it, it's, Jen, lake, let's, make, must, not, panted, please, ride, see, take, that, this, up, us, we, when, yelled, yes, yet

High-Frequency Words

New

hard, or, turn, turns, want, wants

Previously Taught

a, do, I, said, the, to, you, your

Theme 7, Week 2

Chan's Gift (p. 29) accompanies *Lost!*

Decodable Words

New

Sounds for *oo:* book, Books, Brook, cook, cookbook, Nook, notebook, scrapbook, took

Compound Words: cookbook, notebook, scrapbook

Previously Taught

and, asked, at, Bill's, blank, but, can, Chan, Chan's, cost, dimes, gave, get, gift, had, he, his, home, in, it, it's, just, like, likes, made, make, Miss, Mom, much, needed, Nell's, own, pages, picked, she, string, ten, things, up, with, write

High-Frequency Words

Previously Taught

a, I, said, the, to, too, what, you

Theme 7, Week 2

Ann Can't Sleep (p. 37) accompanies *Lost!*

Decodable Words

New

Sounds for *oo:* books, bookcase, good, shook, took, woods

Compound Words: bookcase, raindrops, treetops

Previously Taught

an, and, Ann, Ann's, big, blowing, can't, cheek, creak, Dad, fell, from, gave, glass, going, got, groan, had, he, his, hot, hug, it, kissed, made, Matt, milk, Mom, plan, she, sleep, stuffed, then, this, time, went, wind, yelled

High-Frequency Words

New

afraid, bear, idea

Previously Taught

a, hard, of, the, to, was

Theme 7, Week 2

Rick and Dad Go Camping (p. 45) accompanies *Lost!*

Decodable Words

New

Sounds for *oo:* brook, fishhooks, took, wood

Compound Words: campfire, campsite, fishhooks, upstream

Previously Taught

and, asked, at, ate, back, bags, beans, but, came, camping, catch, Dad, didn't, fish, fished, fishing, five, go, got, heated, in, lots, Mom, no, not, on, packed, poles, Rick, set, sleeping, tent, this, truck, up, we, we've, wide, yelled

High-Frequency Words

New

bears, water

78

(*Rick and Dad Go Camping*, High-Frequency Words continued)
Previously Taught
a, any, are, of, said, the, they, they're, where

Theme 7, Week 3

Clues from Boots (p. 53) accompanies *If You Give a Pig a Pancake.*

Decodable Words

New
Vowel Pairs *oo, ew, ue, ou:* *Boots, food, Drew, threw, clue, clues, Sue, you*

Long *i* (*igh, ight, ie*): *high, goodnight, light, tight, cried, lie*

Previously Taught
and, asked, bed, bowl, did, from, gave, get, go, good, he, his, if, inside, is, it, jumped, just, keeping, know, let, need, nose, on, picked, pushed, ran, see, she, shut, sleep, stick, stood, thank, then, this, trip, up, went, while, will, with

High-Frequency Words

Previously Taught
a, by, do, down, for, I, said, the, to, was, water, what, would

Theme 7, Week 3

Lou's Tooth (p. 61) accompanies *If You Give a Pig a Pancake.*

Decodable Words

New
Vowel Pairs *oo, ew, ue, ou:* *loose, Moon, too, tooth, chew, knew, new, glue, true, group, Lou, Lou's, soup, you*

Long *i* (*igh, ight, ie*): *sighed, right, cried, pie, tried*

Previously Taught
an, and, at, being, big, but, can't, class, didn't, eat, fell, felt, fish, gave, glad, good, had, his, in, is, it's, just, lace, Lee, list, log, look, looked, lunch, make, Miss, Mom, name, nice, not, on, patch, she, shed, show, take, teeth, that, wrote, yet

High-Frequency Words
New
old, shoe, start

Previously Taught
a, any, away, for, have, here, I'll, my, of, said, should, the, to, was, why

Theme 7, Week 3

A Clean Room (p. 69) accompanies *If You Give a Pig a Pancake.*

Decodable Words
New
Vowel Pairs *oo, ew, ue, ou: Boo, boots, broom, room, scooped, chew, new, threw, blue, glue, you*

Long *i (igh, ight, ie): sighed, flashlight, right, lie*

Previously Taught
and, bed, best, bits, blocks, bone, can, clean, cut, Dad, Dad's, desk, did, dimes, five, games, glad, go, good, got, green, hats, his, hung, is, it, job, just, let's, like, lost, mess, missing, Mom's, nice, not, picked, play, raincoat, read, real, she, so, stick, swept, then, this, three, Trish, up, when, with

High-Frequency Words
New
build, pieces, shoes, start, under, very, wear

Previously Taught
a, found, her, here, I'll, now, of, out, paper, said, the, to, was